LIFE, DEATH AND LITIGATION IN THE ATHENIAN AGORA

AMERICAN SCHOOL OF CLASSICAL STUDIES AT ATHENS

1994

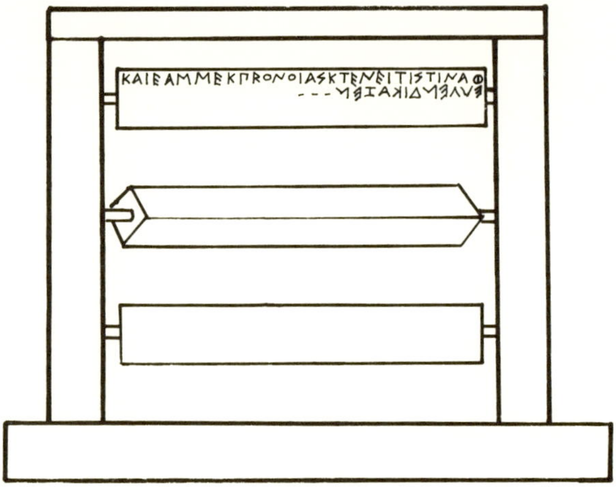

1. Reconstruction of wooden *axones* on which the laws of Solon were recorded in the Stoa Basileios

THAT the Athenian reputation for litigiousness was well earned is clear from the number and variety of extant forensic speeches dealing with every kind of case from assault and battery to murder, from small debts to contested fortunes. Why the Athenians were so eager to go to law, even though lawyers had not yet been invented, is less clear. Certainly some responsibility lies with Solon, the early 6th-century B.C. lawgiver (1), who according to Aristotle (*Ath. Pol.* 9.1) first made it possible "for anyone who wished (*ho boulomenos*) to prosecute on behalf of the wronged." Solon's laws also allowed citizens to appeal a magistrate's decision to a jury of fellow citizens. It was this innovation that gave "most support to the rule of the People. For when the People (*Demos*) have the vote, they have control of the state. Furthermore, because the laws are not written simply and clearly but like the ones on inheritances and heiresses, inevitably there are many disputes, and the lawcourt adjudges all cases, both public and private" (*Ath. Pol.* 9.1–2).

It seems likely that before Solon's time only magistrates and the Court of the Areopagos, composed of ex-magistrates, made judicial decisions. With the institution of the popular court, plantiffs and defendants made their pleas to a jury of their peers. Only murder trials continued to be heard by the Areopagos and other special homicide courts; most cases came before panels (*dikasteria*) of the court of appeal, whose juries could range from 200 to more than 1000 members. The jurors were selected by lot, and this, combined with the large numbers of individuals sitting on even the smallest panels and the random assignment of cases, made juries truly representative and precluded bribery or corruption. Because so many citizens par-

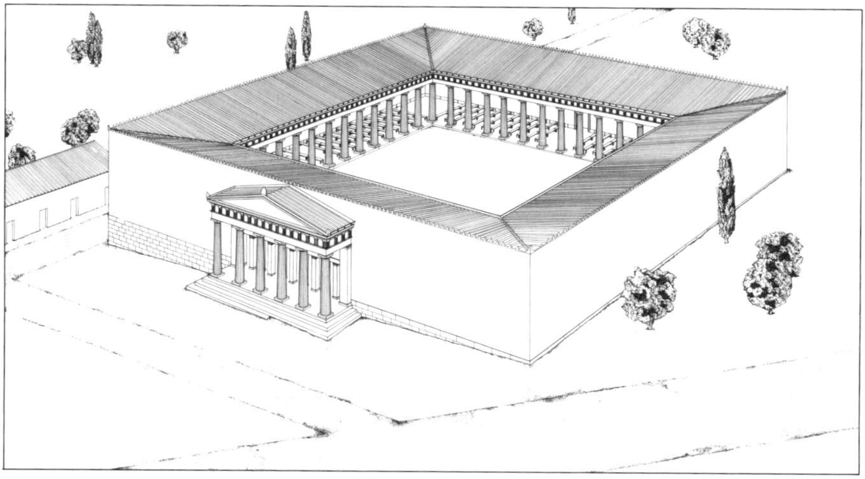

2. Square Peristyle in the northeast corner of the Agora, where many courts met. Late 4th century B.C.

ticipated in jury service, experience and interest in judicial proceedings were sufficiently general to explain the ease and gusto with which Athenians of all sorts prosecuted and defended a variety of lawsuits. Lawsuits were of two general sorts: private cases (*dikai*), in which prosecution was undertaken by the injured party, and public cases (*graphai*), which could be prosecuted in the interest of the community by anyone who wished (*ho boulomenos*). Surprisingly for us, homicide cases were considered private (*dikai phonou*), undoubtedly a remnant of blood-feud morality where it was the family of the deceased that exacted vengeance. Other private cases involved personal loss or damage to body, position, or property. Public cases included accusations of impiety, military desertion, temple robbery, and treachery. A few crimes, like theft, could be prosecuted with either a private or public suit. Most trials were held somewhere in the Agora (2).

All this without lawyers? We do not know how it may have been before the end of the 5th century, although it seems that individual citizens made their pleas in prosecution or defense informally and without special expertise. But after the great teacher of rhetoric, Gorgias, visited Athens in 427 B.C., we begin to have evidence for a new emphasis on rhetoric and intense concern with the techniques of oral presentation and the arts of persuasion. Formal speech writing came into being around this time, and plaintiffs and defendants began to call upon professionals to make their cases. The first such speech writer we know of is Antiphon (born *ca.* 480 B.C.), praised by the historian Thucydides as "one of the best of the Athenians of his time both in planning and speaking" (8.68). Antiphon practiced and taught

3. Practicing the javelin throw. Will this boy look to be sure that the flight path is clear of fellow athletes?

the art of rhetoric; he wrote speeches for actual clients to deliver in court and devised sample cases involving speeches for prosecution and defense to demonstrate different kinds of arguments and techniques of persuasion.

HOMICIDE AND ASSAULT

One of these sample cases (*Tetralogy B*) argued the pro and con of guilt when one boy practicing javelin throws in the gymnasium killed another boy who ran into the javelin's path. The death is accidental but must be avenged, and so responsibility must be fixed. In actual cases like this one the penalty was exile unless or until the families of the victim and killer became reconciled. In Antiphon's example, the fathers are made to show in various, somewhat sophistic ways either how the javelin thrower was guilty of hitting and killing and so must pay the penalty or how the runner was responsible for being hit and killed and so had already paid the penalty (3).

In an actual accidental homicide case, Antiphon wrote a speech (Antiphon 5) for a good citizen who had been selected as Choregos (producer of his tribe's chorus) for the boys' singing competition at the Thargelia (a spring festival to Apollo),

4. Boundary stone of the Agora: "I am a boundary marker of the Agora." Those accused of murder were barred from the public space.

although he was already involved in a lawsuit to impeach a quartet of embezzlers. When one of the boys accidentally died from a drink given him to improve his voice, the embezzlers seized the opportunity to quash the Choregos' case against them by urging the boy's family to prosecute him for murder and so bar him from continuing his own legal action. That was possible because anyone accused of killing was excluded from temples and from the Agora (and consequently from all judicial action therein; 4). But because the case of the dead youth was brought to the King Archon (*archon basileus*), who would preside (5), too late in his term for him to see it through, he was obliged to refuse it, and so the Choregos' prosecution of the embezzlers was successfully carried out. The boy's family, eager to dissociate themselves from the convicted embezzlers, was quickly reconciled with their son's "murderer" in a formal ceremony on the Akropolis and in informal conversation in the Agora. But when Antiphon's client learned of further embezzling and instituted new proceedings, the boy's family was induced by the embezzlers to renew their homicide suit with the new King Archon, thereby revealing, as Antiphon takes pains to show in his speech for the defense, their contempt for the law and

5. Stoa Basileios: the office of the King Archon. The statue in front is probably that of Themis, goddess of Justice.

utter lack of scruples in prosecuting as a murderer a man whom they had already acknowledged to be free of guilt. The civic-minded Choregos seems to have had a good case; it would be interesting to know how the speech writer for the boy's family made the case for the prosecution.

Antiphon also wrote for a young man who was prosecuting his stepmother for the murder of his father (Antiphon 1). As this was an intentional homicide, it was heard by the Court of the Areopagos (6). The father had died, along with a friend, after being served poisoned wine by the friend's female slave. The speech begins with a description of how the stepmother had been caught in a previous poisoning attempt and then claims that she persuaded the slave woman to serve the poisoned wine to her master, saying that it contained a love potion guaranteed to restore his

6. Seat of the Court of the Areopagos (foreground). Homicide courts met in the open air to avoid the transmission of pollution from blood-guilt.

7. A slave woman serving at a banquet. Could she be saying: "Drink up"? And could that cup hold poisoned wine?

affection (7). All this had come out in the interrogation under torture of the slave woman, who had already been executed. (In Athens, evidence given by slaves was only admissible if obtained by torture.) The plaintiff adduces as further proof of his stepmother's guilt her refusal to allow her own slaves to be tortured to provide evidence. Unfortunately, as so often with other recorded speeches for prosecution or defense, we will never know what really occurred or what the verdict was.

Lysias began his speech-writing career less than a decade after Antiphon's death in 411 B.C. (8). Lysias was not an Athenian citizen but a metic (a foreigner living in Athens), whose family was on intimate terms with Sokrates. One of his speeches (Lysias 1), written for Euphiletos (on trial at the Delphinion as a case of justifiable homicide) for killing his wife's seducer, exemplifies Lysias' outstanding talent: the ability to make a speech fit the speaker and present him as speaking simply and

8. Lysias, son of Kephalos and friend of Sokrates

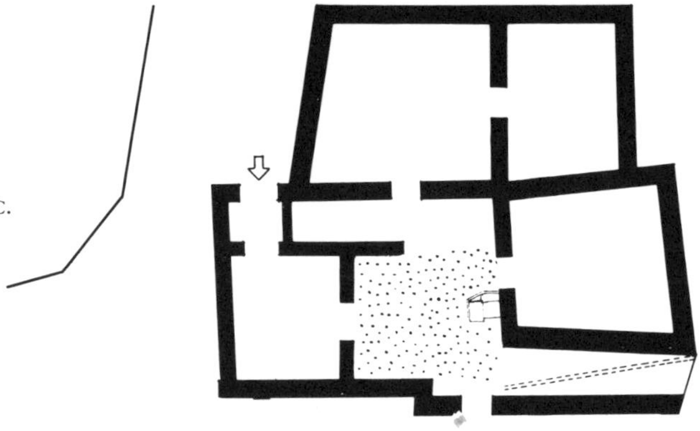

9. Plan of 4th-century B.C. house (C) near the Agora

from the heart. Euphiletos describes the layout of his house (9, 10) in which the location of the women's quarters (ordinarily upstairs) and men's quarters were reversed, so that the mother would be near the well when water was needed for the baby. He tells how his suspicions were aroused one night because he heard the outside door and, when his wife went down to the baby, she later returned wearing makeup. His suspicions were confirmed by information from a woman who had earlier been a victim of the same seducer. With no intention to entrap, he says, but simply taking advantage of the opportunity offered and accompanied by witnesses, he surprised the seducer in the act and killed him. His defense was that he acted only as the agent of the law that exacted death as the penalty for adultery, although in actual fact all that the law said was that for a husband to kill an adulterer was lawful.

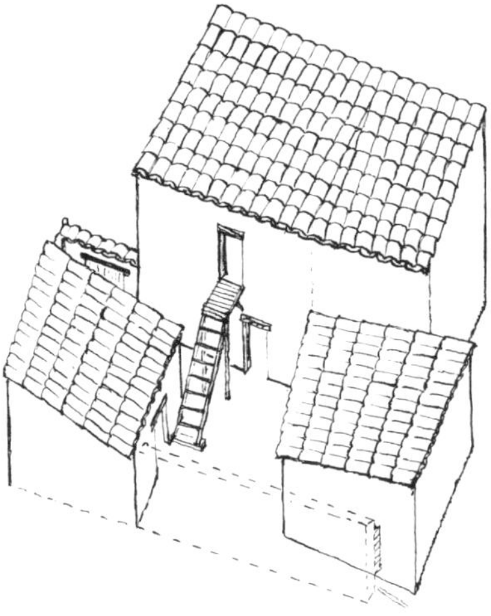

10. Restored drawing of House C to show Euphiletos' arrangements. Leaving her husband, the wife would have come down the wooden staircase to meet her lover when the maid signaled her and provided the necessary excuse by pinching the baby to make him cry.

Cases of wounding with intent to kill, like intentional homicide, were tried by the Areopagos (6). Lysias wrote speeches for the defendants in two such cases (Lysias 2, 3). In each case wounds were inflicted during violent quarrels between prosecutor and defendant, one over a boy, the other over a slave girl. The pleas are largely based on the drunken nature of the encounters which precluded any premeditation. That brawls of this sort were not unusual in Athens is suggested by a prosecution speech written by Demosthenes more than half a century later for Ariston (Demosthenes 54), a young man who brought a suit for assault and battery against an older man named Konon. All that we know about the case and the incident that gave rise to it comes from the agitated and biased account in Ariston's speech.

The Incident. In his narrative the plaintiff Ariston points out the very spot in the Agora where Konon and his sons launched the attack, just opposite the Leokorion (11). "They first stripped me, then tripping me up and pushing me into the mud, they leapt on me and struck me so that they split my lip and closed my eyes; and they left me so badly off that I could neither get up nor speak" (Demosthenes 54.8).

11. Restored drawing of Agora northwest corner: the shrine in the foreground has been tentatively identified as the Leokoreion where Ariston said he was attacked. Stoa Basileios at left; Stoa Poikile at right

12. Beginning of an arbitrators' decision in 367 B.C. These were private arbitrators agreed on by both parties and different from the public arbitrators assigned to act officially in a variety of private cases. Each year the list of public arbitrators was made up of all the men in their sixtieth year, at the end of their liability for military service. The Forty Judges of the Ten Tribes, who were in charge of most private cases, judged matters involving less than ten drachmas but assigned all others to a public arbitrator.

The First Action: Arbitration. Ariston's recovery was slow and painful, and he obviously wanted satisfaction. This was clearly not the kind of quarrel in which both sides could agree to accept the decision of a private arbitrator. So he took his charge to the four judges of Konon's tribe, who passed it on to a public arbitrator (12). At the arbitration meeting Konon used delaying tactics, bringing in irrelevant testimony. To put off the sealing of the evidence (13), he wanted to hand over slaves to give evidence under torture. Ariston seems to have refused to accept the proffered slaves' evidence, and that may have influenced the arbitrator's decision which seems to have favored Konon. Ariston then appealed the arbitrator's verdict.

The Real Action: Court Trial. Both plaintiff and defendant usually spoke twice in a trial. The speech which we have must have been the prosecution's first because

13a. Echinos. Since appeal of the arbitrator's verdict was possible and since only evidence brought forward in the arbitration could be used in any later court action, all the material presented by each side had to be sealed in two hedgehog-shaped jars called *echinoi* (hedgehogs or sea-urchins).

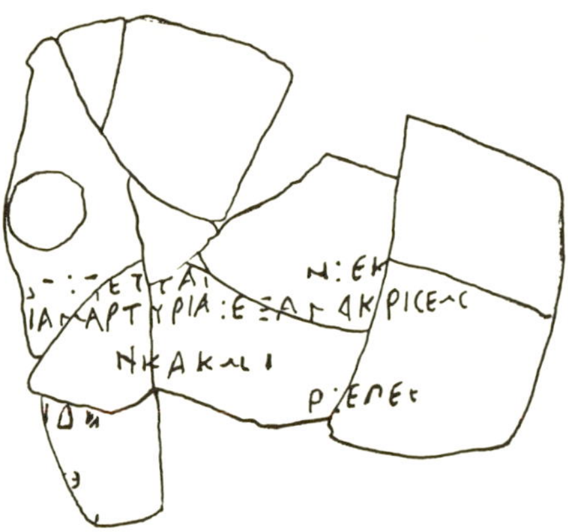

13b. Fragmentary echinos lid inscribed ". . . four . . . from pre-trial . . . of abuse . . . lit[igants] . . ."

after describing the incident it concentrates not on answering any arguments made by the defense but on predicting and attempting to forestall any case that might be made. In discounting Konon's witnesses Ariston contrasts their reputation and bias as fellow drinkers with the impartiality and integrity of his own witnesses, who had simply happened by and testified to his wretched condition. Without making an actual claim, he implies that his witnesses could identify the perpetrators as well. He then continues to undermine the character of both Konon and his witnesses by a variety of innuendoes, ending up with pious representations of his own integrity and expectations that the jurors will defend the injured to discourage wrongdoing. Demosthenes here seems to outdo even Lysias in so presenting the plaintiff's speech that we see him as he must have been: pompous, self-righteous, not "one of the boys" but readier with his tongue than his fists, and a little spiteful.

SHOPKEEPERS AND PUBLIC SCRUTINY

Not only the comparatively well-to-do employed speech writers but even a welfare recipient could seek such help, either expecting outright charity or making the fee contingent on results. In one case (Lysias 24) Lysias has given us a speaking portrait of an individual making much of his crippled state as he indignantly protests the plaintiff's proposal to the Council of 500 (*Boule*) that he be taken off the welfare rolls (for those below the poverty line and too disabled to work; Aristotle, *Ath. Pol.* 49.4). The plaintiff has accused him of being more licentious than needy, pointing to the low company that frequents his little shop (14), which is his only

14. Shoemaker's shop: a relief dedicated by one Dionysios. It would be in such a shop that men gathered to hear and tell the latest news.

source of livelihood (he does not mention what he sells). He replies, "But my shop is no different from the others, nor are those who enter it. For each of you habitually goes, one to the perfume shop, another to the barber shop, one to a shoemaker's shop, or wherever. . . . So if any one of you accuses anyone who comes to me of wickedness, it is clear that he is accusing those who spend time in other men's shops; and if he accuses those, then all Athenians" (Lysias 24.20). This speech is addressed to the Council acting judicially in its administration of the dole and its scrutiny for eligibility of those receiving it.

Another shop in the Agora plays an important role in a speech (*adv. Athenogenem*) written some fifty years later by the orator Hypereides for a farmer probably named [Ep]ikrates (the oration is preserved in a fragmentary state in a papyrus, with the name only partially preserved). Epikrates fancied a son of a slave named Midas, who with his two sons managed a perfume shop for the *metic* Athenogenes, an Egyptian resident in Athens (15). When Epikrates offered to purchase the freedom of the boy, the wily Athenogenes persuaded him to insist that his father and brother be freed also. Athenogenes set the price for all three at 40 minas, throwing in the perfume shop as well. Epikrates, urged on by the Egyptian's mistress, met the price, only to learn that by purchasing the slaves (in order to free them) he had become responsible for any debts they might have. Since their debts turned out to be more than seven times the purchase price, Epikrates and his friends, accosting Athenogenes in the Agora, tried to expose him to public scorn for his sharp practice. Unsuccessful in this, Epikrates entered a suit for damages. His choice of Hypereides as speech writer shows a sudden access of wisdom, for the case needed

15. Perfume shop: red-figured pelike

16. *Phryne before the Tribunal* by Jean-Leon Gerome

all the versatility, polite satire, and barbed wit with which Hypereides was credited by the author of *On the Sublime.* Hypereides was equally famed for having persuaded a jury to acquit the courtesan Phryne of impiety by tearing off her clothes to lay bare her innocence (16). What was the outcome of Epikrates' case we do not know.

Turning back to less scandalous matters, we can see the more sober versatility of the speech writer Lysias in his speeches written again for men being scrutinized (like the cripple) by the Council, but this time for membership in that body (17). Since selection was by allotment, with no guarantee of fitness, the Council reserved to itself the right of refusal. In one case (Lysias 16) Mantitheos, accused of having served in the cavalry under the Thirty Tyrants and so being unfit to act in the democratic Council, defends himself by showing that although his name appeared on lists of prospective cavalrymen, it was not on the list of those who had actually served. In simple and straightforward fashion he tells how he conducted his life, eschewing private vices and serving the public good. At the end, reminiscing about the way in which his ancestors were always engaged in public affairs and noting how much they were respected, he asks, "Who would not be inspired to act and speak on the city's behalf?" (Lysias 16.21).

Lysias' other speech concerning scrutiny by the Council was written for a sitting

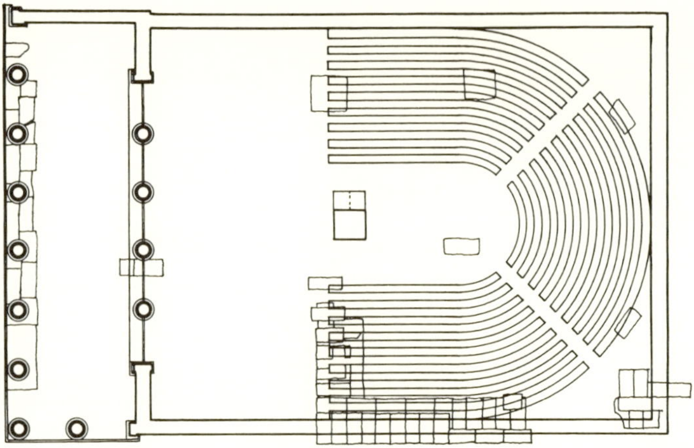

17. New Bouleuterion, built in the late 5th century B.C. Here sat the 500 Councilors, annually allotted, who not only prepared legislation for the Assembly (of all Athenian citizens) but also had a variety of executive and judicial powers.

Council member who charged one Philon of gross unfitness for membership. Not only had he "thought his own safety more important than the common danger of the city" (Lysias 31.7) but he had even taken advantage of the tyranny of the Thirty to rob others; even his mother so mistrusted him that she gave money to an outsider to ensure that she would be buried properly. How could such a man, he asks, be allowed to uphold the democracy he had betrayed and to make laws for others?

FORTUNES AND WILLS

The resident alien Lysias had access to the courts both as a speech writer and in his own person, but unlike his predecessor Antiphon and his successor Demosthenes, as a *metic* he did not have the citizen's privileges of holding office and generally participating in the political life of the city. Isokrates, his younger contemporary and an Athenian citizen, did use his very considerable rhetorical talents in attempts to affect Athenian policy, largely by political pamphleteering, since his speaking voice was weak (18). His greatest interest was in the renewal of the pan-Hellenic unity sparked by the Persian invasion a century before, which he hoped might be accomplished by Hellenic invasion of Persia under a strong leader. His School of Rhetoric was famous throughout Hellas, and, when Queen Artemisia memorialized her husband Mausolos at his death in 353 B.C. with a rhetorical contest, all those who took part were pupils of Isokrates.

18. Isokrates son of Theodoros Erchieus. He owned slaves who were skilled in flute making.

Isokrates wrote comparatively few speeches for individuals to plead their causes in the courts. Two are especially noteworthy because they reflect his pan-Hellenic interests and deal with different aspects of the judicial scene. In one suit (Isokrates 17) the banker Pasion, who was both used and trusted by Demosthenes' father, is accused of failure to return a deposit (19). The plaintiff was the son of a certain

Athenian tetradrachm **Corinthian stater** **Theban stater** **Chian tetradrachm**

1 Ath. tetradr., 17.4 g (4 dr. @ 4.35 g) = 2 Cor. stat., 17.4 g (6 dr. @ 2.9 g)

1¾ Ath. tetradr., 30.45 g (7 dr. @ 4.35 g) = 2½ Theb. stat., 30.5 g (5 dr. @ 6.1 g)

2¼ Ath. tetradr., 39.15 g (9 dr. @ 4.35 g) = 2½ Chian tetradr., 39 g (10 dr. @ 3.9 g)

19. Bankers (*trapezetai*) originally sat at tables (*trapezai*) and changed money. Compare the money-changers' tables in the temple at Jerusalem (*Matthew* 21.12). Most Greek cities had their own mints and coined on various standards.

Sopaios, governor of a province under the King of Bosporos; this son was sent to Athens with two grain ships to sell in order to pay for his education there. No sooner had the son deposited the proceeds from the sale with Pasion the banker than news came that the King of Bosporos had arrested Sopaios for treason and instructed his agents in Athens to seize the son's property and send him home. The son and Pasion conspired to hand over to the agents a small sum as the whole of the son's property. When the agents were satisfied and the son, preparing to go home, went to the bank to reclaim the bulk of his deposit, Pasion refused, denying its existence. The plaintiff's speech details his many unsuccessful efforts to regain his money, among which was a meeting of both parties with torturers at the Hephaisteion (20) to question Pasion's confidential slave. The plaintiff recalls, "I thought it right for them to whip and rack the boy until he seemed to them to tell the truth, but Pasion refused to let the officers seize him and ordered them to question him verbally if they wanted any information"(17.15). Pasion tried every dodge to avoid payment, according to the plaintiff, but his very obvious bias and

20. Hephaisteion, above the west side of the Agora. It is also mentioned as a meeting place for arbitration in Isokrates 17 and [Demosthenes] 33.18.

Pasion's continued good repute suggest that there may have been some question about the justice of his claim.

Isokrates' second "pan-Hellenic" speech (Isokrates 19) was written for a Siphnian whose claims to an inheritance are built up as the persons involved move from island to mainland and back again during a time of unrest in the Aegean (21). The claimant and his deceased friend, Thrasylochos, grew up together on Siphnos, where the latter's father had settled after gaining a fortune by soothsaying throughout Hellas. The soothsayer had deposited much of his fortune on the island of Paros; when trouble broke out there, the claimant managed at considerable risk to retrieve the money for his friend. When they were forced to flee from Siphnos to Melos, Thrasylochos fell ill and begged the claimant to accompany him to Troizen. The claimant and his family moved to Troizen to nurse his friend despite the unhealthfulness of the place, and there the claimant lost both his mother and sister to the plague. Meanwhile Thrasylochos' only brother was killed in Lycia, and again this little group moved, this time to Aigina, where Thrasylochos, feeling his end was near, made a will adopting the claimant and giving him his sister in marriage. Why then did he need to go to court to claim his inheritance? Because a woman came forward claiming to be a daughter of Thrasylochos' father, who, before settling in

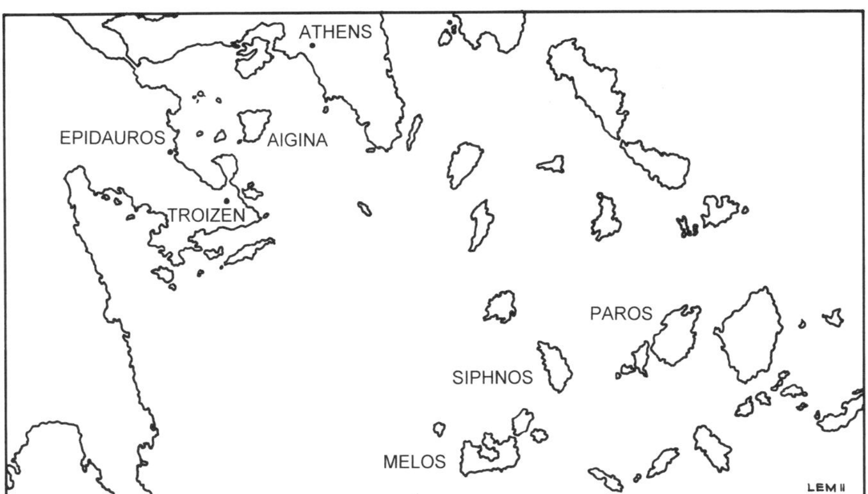

21. The Thrasylochos family in the Aegean, located successively in Siphnos, Paros, Melos, Troizen, and Aigina

Siphnos and fathering Thrasylochos, had been involved with various women in his soothsaying travels. This woman must have had some proof of her relationship, but the speech only tells us what the claimant expected her to argue: that her father would be dishonored if his estate went not to his own flesh and blood but to a stranger adopted by his son. The speaker's answer is that if indeed she was a daughter of the soothsayer, her failure to help his son in all his difficulties made her unfit to inherit from either, while his own devoted service to Thrasylochos, even at bitter cost to himself, gave him closer ties. This is the only case we have that was tried outside Athens, but although the laws referred to are those of Aigina and Siphnos, they seem to be similar to Athenian laws of inheritance.

Much more evidence about adoption, wills, and disputes over inheritance is found in the speeches written by Isaios, a pupil of Isokrates and a teacher of Demosthenes. Isaios seems to have specialized in writing for persons involved in such cases. One speech (Isaios 2) in particular illustrates the complexities of family relationships and inheritance in a society where the absence of offspring often led to the adoption of adults as heirs. The estate in dispute is that of Menekles, who was on intimate terms with Eponymos and his family (22). When Eponymos died, his two sons, having given one sister in marriage to Leukolophos, were happy to give the other sister to Menekles, whose first wife had died childless (23). When this marriage too proved to be infertile, Menekles thought it best to divorce the young woman so that she could marry a younger man. Soon after she had remarried and produced two sons, Menekles decided to adopt one of her brothers (the speaker) to be his heir, thus continuing the close relationship with Eponymos'

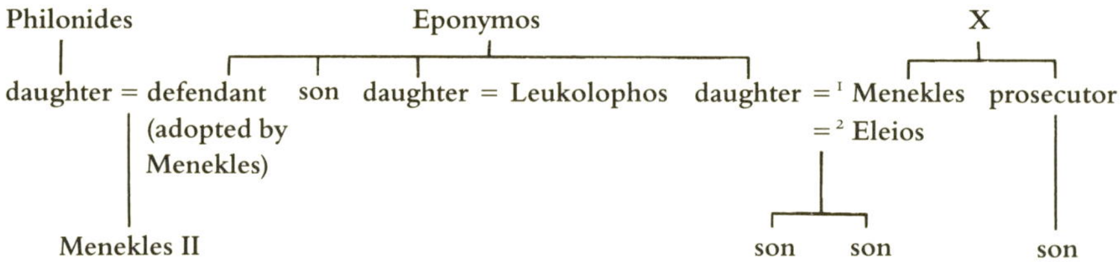

22. Menekles' family and connections. Note the two marriages of Eponymos' second daughter, who was supposed to have unduly influenced her first husband to adopt her brother.

23. A wedding such as Eponymos' sons may have provided for their two sisters. Red-figured pyxis

family. This is the situation as described by the adoptee, in whose interest it obviously was to make the best possible case for the propriety and legality of the adoption.

The prosecutor, Menekles' brother, on the other hand, seems to have charged that the adoption was illegal because Menekles was either of unsound mind or under the influence of a woman at the time. Even so, this is not a simple case of the adoptee defending his right to Menekles' estate. Not at all, for when the prosecutor entered the suit against the adoptee's inheriting, the adoptee's father-in-law Philonides responded with a "witnessing" (*diamartyria*) to the effect that the estate was not subject to a court decision because there was a son (in Athenian law a son, whether genuine or adopted, inherited automatically, nor could anything be willed away from him). This meant then that the prosecutor had first to bring a case of false-witnessing against the father-in-law; only if he won it would he be able to reenter the suit against the adoptee. The present speech, therefore, although spoken by the claimant adoptee to prove his claim to Menekles' estate, is actually in defense of his father-in-law's "witnessing".

The speaker tries to show that the prosecutor is wrong in claiming that Menekles made the adoption under the influence of the sister who had been his wife, for by that time she had had two sons and would have been interested in seeing one of them, rather than her brother, adopted as Menekles' heir. The speaker supports his claim thus: "I, his [adopted] son, took care of Menekles while he lived, both I and my wife, the daughter of this Philonides, and I gave his name to my child, so that his line might not die out, and when he died I buried him in a manner worthy of both him and myself, and I put up a fine monument (24), and I made the ninth-day offerings and did everything else about the tomb as nicely as I could, so that all the townspeople approved" (Isaios 2.36).

There are complications, of course, and some suggestion that the resulting estate was hardly worth claiming, but one suspects that although the plaintiff may well have had a very good case against the speaker for having spent lavishly from the estate while taking such good care of Menekles, he could only interfere by proving the adoption illegal.

Still more complicated is another case (Isaios 10) for which Isaios' expertise was required, involving as it did both adoption and the situation in which the only

24. This stone marking a burial reads: "Boundary of the monument: 12 feet along the road; 16 feet in." This seems very modest compared to what Isaios' client says he did for his adopted father Menekles.

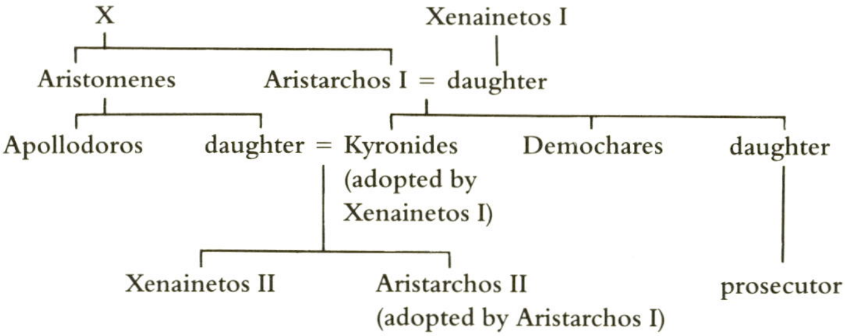

25. Aristarchos' family and connections

surviving child of the deceased was female. One Xenainetos, having only a daughter, adopted her elder son Kyronides by her husband Aristarchos, taking him out of his father's line and leaving the younger son Demochares to carry it on (25). This younger son died soon after his father, so that only a daughter was left. She could not herself inherit; the expected thing was for a close male relative to marry her and manage the property for their children to carry on the line. But no male relative claimed her, and Aristarchos' line seems to have been carried on by the posthumously(?) adopted second son of Kyronides (Aristarchos II). It looks very much as if the intent was to concentrate the property of both Xenainetos and Aristarchos in one family.

The daughter who should have been Aristarchos' "heiress" was married to an outsider and had a son who, as the speaker in this oration, claims to be the true heir of his mother's father Aristarchos. His case was crippled from the start by an Athenian law which required that since his mother was not married to a male relative he was not in Aristarchos I's line and so the only relationship on which he could base his claim was his mother's sistership to Aristarchos II, by virtue of the latter's adoption by Aristarchos I. The speaker thus had to plead not as his grandfather's heir but as a rival of his natural cousin, who was also his uncle by adoption as the adopted heir of that grandfather. To complicate matters still more, since Aristarchos II had recently died in battle, the defendant in this case was his brother Xenainetos II. Actually, it is likely that it was that death that encouraged the plaintiff to try for a share in his estate, since property is always easier to claim when it is passing from one person to others than when it is firmly in someone's possession.

At any rate, one of the speaker's main arguments is the questionable nature of the adoption of Aristarchos II: it could not have been made by Aristarchos I, since he could not disinherit his natural son Demochares who was still alive at his death, and how could it have been made by Kyronides who no longer belonged to Aristarchos' family? We can only guess that Kyronides had somehow restored the fortunes of Aristarchos' house and so had the right to "nominate" the heir. One other argument shows the speaker's pique at the thought that Xenainetos II, who was ending up with the property of both houses, was squandering it on pretty boys (26).

26. Isaios' client claimed that an estate rightfully his was being spent in this kind of pursuit. Red-figured pelike

27. Demosthenes, son of Demosthenes Paianieus

WHAT'S IN A NAME?

Demosthenes, the most renowned Athenian political orator, was also active in a variety of private cases both of his own and of his clients (27). King Philip of Macedon spoke of him with admiration: "I myself, if I had heard Demosthenes speak, would have chosen him general to carry on the war against me." But a rival Athenian orator, Demades, characterized him as "a little man made up of syllables and a tongue."

One of Demosthenes' clients was a Mantitheos who was almost certainly the grandson of the virtuous Mantitheos for whom Lysias wrote, defending his fitness to serve in the Council (see above, p. 13). This case (Demosthenes 39) is most instructive for the light it sheds on the importance of names in ancient Athens. Mantitheos had a half-brother, Boiotos, who claimed that *his* name was Mantitheos Mantiou (son of Mantias) Thorikios (of Thorikos deme or township). For two

28. Typical bronze nameplate issued to a citizen for use in allotments to courts and also to offices: "Demophanes Phil. . . . /Kephisieus." In his suit Mantitheos says, "Unless some mark should be applied to the bronze, people will not know to which of us it belongs."

men in Athens to have the same name created a serious and awkward situation, especially since both allotment to certain offices and assignment of various taxes were by name alone (28). Which of two men having the same name could claim the office or evade the tax? Therefore, for Mantitheos Mantiou Thorikios to sue Boiotos for calling himself Mantitheos Mantiou Thorikios seems only right and logical. But because we know that Boiotos won the case, presumably because the jury's verdict was based on facts rather than eloquence, we are in a better position than usual to question the case as presented in the extant speech.

Mantitheos tells us that a son of a woman named Plangon had entered a suit against his father Mantias, to force him to acknowledge her boy as his son. Mantias wanted to avoid a trial in which his political enemies might do him harm and so planned to do a deal with Plangon before the arbitrator: he would challenge her to swear an oath that he was the father but at the same time pay her a large sum to refuse the challenge. But at the meeting with the arbitrator Plangon tricked him and *did* swear the oath, so that he was forced to acknowledge Plangon's son and register him in his clan. Mantias registered him in the clan under the name Boiotos. But Mantias died before registering Boiotos in his deme. Boiotos did that himself but used the name Mantitheos. Despite this apparent usurpation of the name, the verdict in Boiotos' favor makes it likely that Plangon had been Mantias' first wife but that because he had suspected that the boy was not his, he divorced her and, having married again, fathered the plaintiff Mantitheos. When Mantias was tricked by Plangon into acknowledging her son, it was that son who by virtue of seniority had the right to his paternal grandfather's name.

In conclusion, Mantitheos reminds the court of the regular jurors' oath, which has been reconstructed by modern scholars from bits and pieces in the ancient sources: "I will vote in accordance with the laws and decrees of the *Demos* of the Athenians and the Council of 500. In cases not covered by laws I will vote in accordance with what is most just without favor or malice. I will hear both the plaintiff and defendant equally, and I will vote about the matter at issue (29). I swear by Zeus, Poseidon, Demeter and invoke destruction upon myself and my house if I violate this oath in any way, but many blessings if I keep it" (Demosthenes 23.96;24.149;39.39–40;57.63).

29. Bronze ballots with which jurors voted; the large letter epsilon indicates tribe (?), small letters say "official vote". The solid hub is for acquittal, the hollow hub for condemnation.

TAX DODGERS AND PROPERTY DISPUTES

Disputes over the Athenian very special form of "income tax" gave rise to judicial action. The richest men in Athens each year were assigned "liturgies" of various sorts: providing funds to equip a trireme or warship (*trierarchia*), or to train a chorus (*choregia*), or to prepay the war-tax. A man might be excused if he had held a liturgy the previous year; the only other way out was by a process called *antidosis*, that is,

30. Mortgage stone indicating that the property was not free and clear: "Boundary of house sold, with right of redemption, to the deme Kerameis, 3,000 drachmas"

an exchange: the man assigned the liturgy could challenge another, whom he thought better able to afford it, either to take over the liturgy or to exchange properties. In the Demosthenic corpus, but probably not by Demosthenes, is a speech (Demosthenes 42) in which X charges that the Phainippos whom he had challenged to such an exchange of property had both failed to turn in to the magistrate the required inventory of his estate and started to remove and conceal some of his property. Phainippos had apparently countered with an accusation about the inaccuracy of X's inventory and insisted that part of his property was mortgaged. But X declared that there were no mortgage stones to be seen marking the property (30). Apparently it was a competition between men with different sources of wealth, X exaggerating Phainippos' income from farm produce and Phainippos countering with the great profits X had received from the silver mines. It was up to the court to decide which of the two was richer and so responsible for the liturgy.

Demosthenes initiated several lawsuits on his own behalf. Coming of age at eighteen, he sued his guardian, Aphobos, for mismanagement of his estate and was awarded ten talents in damages. Aphobos' response was to move to Megara, disposing as he could of his property. When Demosthenes attempted to seize a farm worth one talent in partial payment of the damages, he was stopped by Onetor, who, having given his sister in marriage to Aphobos along with a dowry, asserted that the farm had been made over to him by Aphobos in the usual fashion as security to guarantee the restitution of the dowry in case of divorce (31). Onetor further claimed that Aphobos had divorced his sister without restoring the dowry so that

31. Example of stone recording a dowry pledge: "Boundary of house as valuation on the dowry for Patrokleia, daughter of Pantenor Phrearrios, 1,500 drachmas"

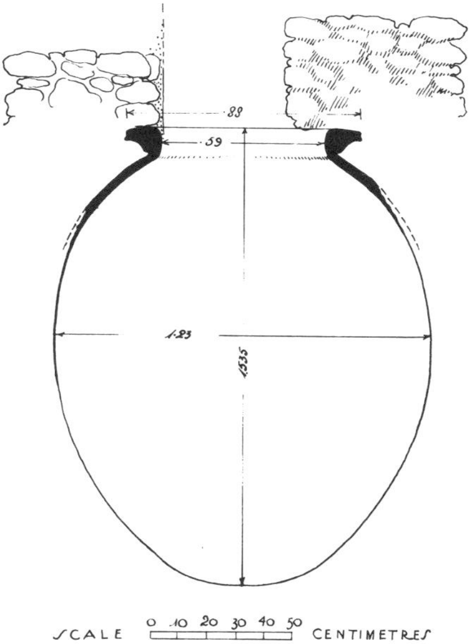

32. Aphobos left behind only property difficult to move, like this storage jar set in the ground (from a house near the Areopagus).

the farm was now his. Demosthenes entered a suit of ejectment against Onetor (Demosthenes 30), contending that Aphobos and Onetor had conspired together to appropriate the property, that the dowry was never paid, and that the divorce was a fiction. Furthermore, Aphobos clearly regarded the farm as forfeit to Demosthenes and not as security since he had removed from it everything of value except the large storage jars set into the ground (32).

BROKEN CONTRACTS

Financial transactions were a rich source of litigation, particularly those dealing with bottomry (lending money on ships and cargos) and trade. One case (Demosthenes 56) involved two Athenians lending 3000 drachmas (33) to Dionysodoros and Parmeniskos, taking their ship as collateral, with the specific agreement that, on the return of the ship from Egypt to Athens, the principal would be repaid along with interest on both voyages (interest on nautical loans ranged from 20 to 33⅓ percent depending on risk). It was understood that if the ship was lost the debt would be canceled, but if the borrowers failed to keep to the agreement, they were liable for double the principal. Dareios, one of the lenders, is the speaker in this suit for damages brought against Dionysodoros, since the ship failed to return to Athens but sold its cargo of grain in Rhodes. This was sharp dealing on the part of the borrowers: with Parmeniskos on the ship and Dionysodoros in Athens, when the price of grain in Athens fell, Dionysodoros could write to Parmeniskos at Rhodes, where the ship would put in, instructing him to sell the grain there to make a greater profit. Since it was against Athenian law for Athenian bottoms to carry grain to other ports, this involved not only the borrowers but also the lenders in illegal action. Moreover, the ship then proceeded to trade back and forth between Rhodes and Egypt, although Dionysodoros asserted that the grain had to be sold in Rhodes because the ship had suffered damage. Dareios maintained that the contract was broken and the borrowers owed double the loan, but he was willing to submit the case to arbitration by men knowledgable in sea-going trade. According to him, Dionysodoros refused to do anything more than pay the principal and the interest as far as Rhodes. Perhaps if we had the speech which some other speech writer wrote for Dionysodoros, we would find that he did not have a monopoly on sharp practice, but we might still not know how the jury voted. Dareios' final appeal to the jury was for a vote in his favor as a way to discourage the kind of skulduggery that resulted in scarcity of grain in the Athenian market, presumably a telling point for bread-eating jurors.

Both more complicated and more dramatic is the case (Demosthenes 35) in which Androkles lent to Artemon of Phaselis "3000 drachmas to sail from Athens to Mende or Skione and from there to the Bosporos and, if they wish, on the left coast up to Borysthenes, and back to Athens at interest of 22 percent, but if they sail out after the rising of [the star] Arktouros from Pontos to Hieron, at 30 percent, on security of 3000 jars of Mendean wine which will be conveyed from Mende or Skione in the twenty-oared boat skippered by Hyblesios. . . . And they will bring back goods from Pontos as return cargo to Athens in the same boat. When the

1 talent = 60 mnas = 6,000 drachmas
1 mna = 100 drachmas
1 drachma = 6 obols
1 obol = 8 chalks
4th-century B.C. minimum daily wage: 3 obols

33. Athenian monetary units and minimum daily wage in the 4th century B.C.

34. Mendean wine amphora: height 0.645 m.; maximum diameter 0.389 m.; capacity 23.325 liters. Three thousand such amphoras full of wine would weigh about 130 tons, which was the carrying capacity of an average merchant ship in the later 4th century B.C.

goods are safe in Athens, the borrowers will pay back to the lenders the amount accrued according to the contract within twenty days after their return to Athens, complete except for anything jettisoned which all the passengers have voted in common to throw out, and if they paid anything to hostile forces." When Artemon died without paying back the debt, Androkles sued his brother Lakritos as Artemon's heir and because he had verbally agreed to be his guarantor. But Lakritos put in a special plea to bar the suit because he was not written into the contract and because, having renounced his brother's estate, he was also relieved of its debts. Androkles' reply is to that special plea, but it recounts all his complaints: Artemon had shipped only 450 jars of wine instead of 3000 (34); he raised another loan on the same collateral; he did not bring back cargo from Pontos; and the ship returned not to the Peiraeus but to Thieves' Harbor, and so on.

Androkles wound up his defense against Lakritos' special plea with the question: how are lenders to carry on their profession and facilitate the trade so necessary to Athens if they have no recourse to justice when contracts are broken?

This sampling of court cases from the late 5th to the late 4th century B.C. shows some of the variety and complexity of ancient Athenian litigation as well as the part it played in everyday life. It also does something to explain the bitter remark of Hypereides (frg. 19.5): "Orators are like snakes; all are hateful though some of them, the adders, are harsh to men, while others, the brown snakes, eat adders."

The wonder is how such a judicial system could work, when almost everyone involved, except perhaps the speech writers, was a rank amateur. The speech writers may have served some of the functions of lawyers for the prosecution and defense, but there was no presiding judge learned in the law who could interpret it for the jury. There was only a jury of ordinary citizens, chosen by allotment and so large as to be truly representative and thus generally addressed as "Men of Athens", who were expected to judge matters of law as well as matters of fact. The multiplicity of laws not only increased the difficulties of the jury's decision but also presented the potential litigant with bewildering choices. One defendant notes that there are

> laws which deal specifically with every kind of offense. If someone commits a religious offense, there is public prosecution before the King Archon. If he mistreats his parents, the Archon sits on his case. . . . Likewise for every other offense you have established laws, magistrates and courts, all suited to each (Hypereides, *pro Euxenippou* 5–7).

A prosecutor lists ways in which the law militates against the escalation of violence:

> There are cases of slander, and they say that these were instituted so that men may not be led on, while insulting each other, to blows. Again there are cases of assault and battery; these are so that no one when he finds he is weaker may resort to a stone or anything such but wait for justice from the law; and there are cases of wounding, so that murder may not result from this (Demosthenes 54.17–18).

There are laws of succession concerning inheritance:

> Whoever dies intestate, if he leaves female children, the estate goes with them; if not, the following come into possession: if there are brothers by the same father [they come into possession], and if there are sons of the natural brothers, to take their father's share, and if there are no brothers or sons of brothers . . . (Demosthenes 43.51). The listing goes on to more remote relatives.

Even funerals were regulated (35):

> Mourners were required to lay out the dead inside, however one wishes. To carry out the corpse for burial the next day before the sun rises. The men to walk before, the women behind (Demosthenes 43.62).

35. Mourners tending grave monuments: white-ground lekythos

There was even a law equating corruption of the judicial process with overthrow of the government:

> If anyone conspires or helps to corrupt the Heliaia or any one of the courts at Athens or the Council, either giving or receiving money, or forms an association for the overthrow of the democracy, . . . of these things there are indictments to the Thesmothetes [junior archons] by anyone wishing (Demosthenes 46.26).

As is obvious from the laws, there were magistrates to carry them out, but these, like the jurymen, were mostly allotted, served for a limited term, and often served in boards of ten, presumably to broaden representation and share responsibility. In addition, every citizen was responsible for bringing malefactors to justice in a variety of public cases, as the orator Lykourgos notes:

> For there are three things most important in guarding and preserving the democracy and the city's prosperity: first, the system of laws; second, the vote of the jurors; and third, the arraignment delivering offenses to them. For it is the nature of the law to state what must not be done, of the accuser to indicate those liable to penalties under the law, and of the jurors to punish those pointed out to them by the other two, so that neither the law nor the jurors' vote avails without a prosecutor who will hand wrongdoers over to them (*adv. Leocratem* 3–4).

The system, perhaps not very efficient (as democracy rarely is), did work, but despite built-in checks and balances, there were abuses. Major ones were the practice of sycophancy or informing and the use of litigation for gain or other advantage. Other abuses might include indiscriminate torture of slave witnesses, excessive appeals to the jury, exaggeration of claims, and rhetorical ploys of one sort or another. One has only to read a series of speeches, whether for the prosecution or the defense, to find a variety of commonplaces used over and over again. The speaker is almost always young or inexperienced and pitted against one whose sharp practice is well known; the speaker has been both a virtuous citizen and a benefactor of society with various liturgies, while his opponent has refused to use his ill-gotten gains to serve the state. Always the klepsydra (water clock that timed the speeches; 36) prevented one from presenting one's case adequately, even though it could be stopped for the reading of laws or the testimony of witnesses. And frequently litigants felt it necessary to instruct the jurors concerning the dire results of a contrary vote which would set a precedent for rampant crime in the streets.

Certainly the orations, which are our source for court activity in Athens, combine the personal passions of defendants and prosecutors with the rhetorical arts of the speech writers. In life as in literature, the Athenians' penchant for drama is clearly seen. Tragedies and comedies competed in the Theater of Dionysos only twice a year, but on the 200 or so days when the courts met, it was possible for anyone to speak a part or judge a winner.

36. Model of water clock (*klepsydra*) set up to show the method of timing. This vessel is marked "(Property of) the tribe Antiochis: two *choes* [*ca.* 7 quarts]".